SIMPLE ETIQUETTE IN
turkey

WELCOME TO ASIA

ILLUSTRATED BY
IRENE SANDERSON

SIMPLE ETIQUETTE IN turkey

By
David Shankland

Simple Books Ltd
Sandgate, Folkestone, Kent, England

SIMPLE ETIQUETTE IN TURKEY

Simple Books Ltd
Knoll House, 35 The Crescent,
Sandgate, Folkestone, Kent, England CT20 3EE

First published 1992
© Simple Books Ltd

ISBN 1-873411-00-6

British Library Cataloguing in Publication Data

**A CIP catalogue record for this book
is available from the British Library**

Distributed in the USA & Canada by:
THE TALMAN COMPANY, INC
150 Fifth Avenue
New York, NY 10011

Photoset in Souvenir Light 11 on 12pt
by Visual Typesetting, Harrow, Middlesex
Printed in England by BPCC Wheatons Ltd., Exeter

Contents

ACKNOWLEDGEMENTS

My deepest thanks are due to the Turkish people, for the warmth with which they have discussed their ways and customs with me over the years. I would also thank my cousin, Hugh Shankland, for suggesting that I write this account. I am grateful to Professor Paul Stirling and Cemil Bezmen, who have made careful comments on the manuscript. Of course, any mistakes are my responsibility alone.

Foreword

For centuries Turkey has fascinated Western travellers. On their return, many have written books telling of the marvels of Istanbul (Constantinople), the glories of the Sultan's court and the strength of his army. Turkey retains its power to delight the visitor. But that very power is also a source of confusion. The language is strange, with few familair words. Friendships are made and lost through ways not apparent. Business arrangements are agreed then fall through for no obvious reason. In short, whilst in Turkey, the visitor cannot but suspect that the rules of etiquette are very different from those he or she is used to.

With care, these differences can be overcome. Certain factors are of great importance when trying to empathise with Turkish life; the Republican heritage, the depth of the Islamic culture, the pattern of social relations and the long tradition of hospitality. This book has been written to highlight these factors, so that moments when you say 'That is not what I meant at all!' occur as rarely as possible.

DAVID SHANKLAND
January 1992

there are 40 million sheep in Turkey

Introduction

Even on the briefest trip to Turkey the visitor will be struck by the name Kemal Atatürk. His picture hangs in shops, work places and government buildings. On national holidays his portrait is suspended high from office blocks. Every town square has his statue. Roads, stadiums, sports halls, schools, even towers and dams are named after him. Lessons on his life are compulsory in schools, reputations are made out of scholarly dissertations on his writings.

It would be quite mistaken to regard this veneration as imposed by the government. Modern Turkey was formed out of the Ottoman Empire between 1918 and 1926, and Atatürk was its first president. The institutions and ideals which he created remain substantially unchanged to this day. Through them Turks experience the elements of a modern Western nation: national ballet and opera companies, national museums and libraries, universities and learned bodies, and a democratic parliament; the Grand National Assembly.

RELIGION

Inside a mosque

Part of Atatürk's programme of reforms was devoted to making Turkey secular, that is to say he separated governing the country from religious doctrine. The present-day legal system is based on a combination of the Swiss, German and Italian codes, and a person's private beliefs are distinguished from his business or official transactions. Nevertheless, evidence of the country's Islamic character is all around, and etiquette might be said to begin with respecting its customs.

Turks, like other Islamic peoples, pray in a mosque (*cami*). Non-Muslims are always welcome, but it is polite to wait until a service has ended before entering. Shoes must be taken off and only put on again after leaving the mosque. Whilst inside women are usually asked to cover their heads with a scarf, and both men and women must be decently dressed.

Tourists are free to explore the mosque. Usually photography is permitted. They must not, however, approach the covered galleries which line the rear of the interior (these are reserved for Muslim women) nor the *mihrab*, the niche facing Mecca from which the mosque official, the *imam*, leads the prayer. If the *imam* has welcomed you to the mosque, or guided you around it, then he will expect a tip. The equivalent of £1 ($1.70) is sufficient. This he does not put into his own pocket, but into a fund for the mosque's upkeep.

For one month of the year, *Ramazan*, all believers fast during the hours of daylight. From dawn until sunset they do not drink, eat, or smoke. Most people are tolerant of a foreigner's normal habits, but it puts great strain on those who are fasting if others eat in front of them. During this period restaurants are often screened so that they cannot be seen from the street, and some may be closed during the day. Throughout the month, try to avoid eating in public places.

It is not considered polite to enquire as to a person's religious belief, and unless the subject is brought up it is safe to assume that one's partner in conversation is not fanatical but respectful of the country's religious traditions. Also bear in mind the admiration for Atatürk. A row ensued recently when an American sailor,

.. a synthesis .. between the Muslim and Western worlds

after a night out in a small port in the south, relieved himself over a statue of the great man. The locals were only prevented from lynching the sailor by the police, who were roundly abused for their lack of patriotism.

If Islam and the labels of modern nationhood are respected the visitor can be assured of making new friends, and of delightfully varied experiences; moving from mosque to art gallery, bazaar to shop, concert hall to traditional wedding, continually struck by the way a synthesis appears to have been achieved between the Muslim and Western worlds.

A NOTE ON MONEY

The Turkish unit of currency is the Lira (TL). In February 1992 the Lira was approximately 10,000 to the pound and 6,000 to the dollar. Inflation [at the time of writing] is high, about seventy per cent a year. Visitors are advised to wait until their arrival in Turkey before changing money, and then in small quantities.

For tourists, any surplus lira are freely changeable back into Western currencies. Keep all exchange receipts so that if necessary you can prove you did not obtain them on the black market.

Lira

PRONOUNCING THE LANGUAGE

The Turkish language is written in Roman script, and words are pronounced just as they would be in English with the following exceptions:

ı said as is the 'o' in woman;

ç said as is the 'ch' in church;

c said as is the 'j' in jam;

ö said as is the *'eu'* in the French *veut*.

ş said as is the 'sh' in wish;

ğ said as is the 'y' in yellow, lengthens the preceding vowel;

ü said as is the *'u'* in the French *rue*;

Turkish never runs two consonants together, thus *kütüphane*, library, is pronounced kütüp-hane, with a clearly marked 'h'.

Being a Guest

Turkish Tea - black

Turkish people tend to feel personally responsible for the success of a visitor's stay. Just after I arrived for the first time, for example, I inadvertently plugged the telephone into the electricity socket. Not knowing where to go to have the charred item repaired, I got into a taxi and showed it to the driver. He took me to the main telecommunications building, whereupon the doorman led me to a room where repair men were relaxing, and amid laughter they replaced the blown circuits. I have heard of many similar examples of kindness.

For this reason if someone comes up and asks if they can direct you anywhere, hesitate before replying. Except in the traditional tourists areas of a city such queries are usually genuine and a hasty 'no!' may give offence where none was meant. Equally, they will be delighted if you make the first move and try to make contact with them.

One of the first ways of doing this is to accept a glass of tea, *çay*. Tea is served black with several lumps of sugar at the side of the glass, and drunk in great quantities throughout the country. It may be offered in a *kahve*, literally 'coffee-house' (which, as coffee is hardly drunk in them, is rather mis-named) or in banks, civil service offices, and shops. Once you have had enough it is quite in order to refuse because they themselves sometimes find they are drinking too much.

Language need not be an insurmountable barrier. It is easy to pick up a few words of Turkish, sufficient at least to show your friendly intent, and there are enough English speakers in the major centres who could deal with a translation problem if need be. Useful words are *merhaba*, hello; *evet*, yes; *hayır*, no; *teşekkür ederim*, thank-you. A simpler way of saying thank-you is *sağ ol*! Health be! An absolutely essential word is *yok*! *Yok* is used everywhere to signify none, not any, or an emphatic no.

The Turkish people are sometimes regarded as being dour. This reputation may in part be due to their habit of indicating 'no' by raising the eyebrows, clicking the tongue, tilting the head back, or a combination of all three. If you have asked a question, and not apparently had a response, look carefully to see whether the person you asked is raising his or her eyebrows. Sometimes the signs can be almost imperceptible.

Sometimes the signs can be almost imperceptible.

ON BEING INVITED TO STAY

It is very possible that soon after your arrival you will be invited to stay in someone's home. Such generosity is found throughout Turkey, among rich and poor. Whilst deciding whether to accept there are some pros and cons to consider.

Traditionally, a guest has to be very closely looked after, their wishes anticipated, and all their needs attended to. The invitation may be made more from a desire to please, or out of a feeling of duty, than actually wanting to take on the considerable burden of being a host.

A guest also has obligations. In accepting the invitation, you are placing yourself under the responsibility of the hosts, and should not go against their wishes whilst staying with them. There is a saying which illustrates this, *ev sahibi sultandır*, the host is sultan!

It is a point of honour that guests should not spend any money. If you find offers to pay are repeatedly refused, do not persist. Where we would try to recompense a host by reciprocating fairly quickly, for example when buying drinks, usually they would do so over a much longer period. According to their rules, first the host must have a chance to display his or her generosity, and only later does the guest attempt to repay. It would be quite acceptable to send a gift after returning home, or on a subsequent visit to bring presents with you.

At home

To have guests is a way of increasing one's status, therefore you may receive other invitations from your host's neighbours in the community. If you genuinely wish to stay in a different home in the same vicinity it is better to do so on your next visit, so as not to insult your present host.

ON ENTERING

If in a town, and with a woman who appears Westernised, then a man should step back to allow her through first. If in a village then the man must step through the door before the woman. This is important because in many villages a woman is brought up never to cross a man's path on the grounds that it brings bad luck, *uğur kesme*. It may cause acute embarrassment if a man insists that the woman enters before him.

A town family group

GREETINGS

Be prepared as you enter a strange house for the greeting *hoş geldiniz*, welcome! The correct reply is *hoş bulduk*, well-found! As each new person comes into the room he or she will repeat the greeting, and shake your hand. If a person is much younger than you he may kiss your hand, and press it to his forehead. If the new arrival is an elderly man, then it is polite to stand up for him.

On parting, those leaving say *Allaha ısmarladık*, 'we have consigned ourselves to God', or more simply, *iyi günler*, 'good day'. Those not leaving respond *güle güle*, 'go smilingly'. Note that the party leaving speaks first, and the 'go smilingly' is a reply to their farewell. If, as you are leaving, you repeat your 'good day' then those staying will repeat 'go smilingly', and you may find yourself in a continuous cycle of goodbyes.

2

Eating and Drinking

Smyrne: decorative relief end of (17

In Ottoman Art, gardens often appear as an image of heaven. The love of gardens has remained, and in the summer picnics in orchards and beauty spots are very popular. Picnics are always held in a very leisurely fashion and are a delightful way to experience Turkish life. The food will be absolutely fresh. There will be no pork, which is forbidden by the Koran, but yoghurt, honey, bread, salad, steak and fruit.

Turkish people also enjoy eating outdoors in towns. Most restaurants have a garden in which diners may continue to sit after it gets dark. Usually a meal begins with starters, *meze*. These may be either cold or hot. Among cold starters are yoghurt, olives, stuffed peppers, puréed aubergine, goat's and sheep's cheese, and many varieties of salad. Among hot starters most common are various sautéed meats and *börek*, pastry stuffed with cheese, meat, spinach or mushroom. After this comes the main course, usually roasted or grilled meat, often served with rice, tomato, and salads. All savoury food is accompanied by bread. The sweet may consist of pastries soaked in syrup, or fruit. Coffee comes black, in small cups. If you wish it plain you may ask for *sade*, if with sugar *şekerli*.

Turkish restaurant.

Such a rich and varied menu is quite normal. The meal may well last from the early evening until late at night. In your conversation it is better not to raise problems of ethnic minorities, religion, or politics in Turkey until you know your hosts well. They, however, may ask you detailed questions on contemporary affairs, Western governments, theory of democracy, religion, law, the Common Market, and the way Turkey is regarded by the West. This last point is a very sensitive topic, and you may need to reassure your hosts several times of the goodwill your country holds for them.

Meals are usually accompanied by alcohol

DRINK

Meals in the evening are usually accompanied by alcohol. The national drink is *raki*, a strong spirit somewhat similar to ouzo, which is mixed with water until it turns cloudy. Beer is drunk all over Turkey. Wine tends to be found only in the urban areas. It is made locally and is quite palatable. Some people condemn alcohol on religious grounds, but it is drunk by many, though not to excess, for it is seen as shameful to be drunk.

PAYMENT

If you have just arrived in Turkey, it would be quite wrong for you to pay for the meal. If you have had time to get to know the people with whom you are dining, it may be possible to offer, extremely tactfully, to pay. If they refuse, but you really would like to buy the meal, then a possible solution is to pay the waiter discreetly, in such a way that your actions are not apparent to the rest of the company. This is an established custom, and the waiter will realise what you are doing. Service is included in the bill, but on top of this in the more expensive restaurants it is normal to add between five and ten per cent (always in cash) for the waiter.

3

Social Relations

Taking tea

Most people have a number of close friends, and an enormous number of acquaintances, *arkadaş*. Whenever a favour is required it is to these that they turn. If they need a seat in a bus when it is declared full, they phone up an *arkadaş* who works for the bus company and ask him or her to find a seat for them. If a hotel is full and a few more rooms need to be found then they turn to a fellow proprietor whom they have helped in the past. If they cannot help someone who asks for advice then they telephone an acquaintance and pass them along. Exchanges of aid are an inescapable part of life in Turkey.

They do not just affect private life. Positions in the civil service, local and national government, and key roles within political parties are often allocated through personal contacts. Such ties are also extremely significant in business, where having friends among the local officials and politicians may be vital in order to win contracts, or see projects through.

Thus a foreigner is entering a society in which people from the smallest village to the capital see interaction in far more personal terms than in Northern Europe. In Turkey whom you know is at least as important as what you know.

INTRODUCTION

It helps enormously to have letters of introduction from a person who is familiar to those you are introducing yourself to. If you have a particular purpose you should have letters from someone in an official position explaining your background and reason for being in Turkey. These should have as many large, official-looking stamps as possible. If you wish to get something done the very worst way to go about it is to approach the person concerned with no more than a passport to introduce yourself.

SHOWING RESPECT

At all times, Turkish people are careful to act according to the appropriate degree of respect, *saygı*. The respect an individual commands generally depends on his age, wealth, contacts, and the position he holds in his profession. Also, a father expects to receive respect from his children, wife, and relatives born in a later generation. Failure to show the correct amount of respect is *ayıp*, shameful. Allowances are made for foreigners, but there are a few simple points which, once observed, make life easier.

Respect

Respect is shown to others principally by allowing them to speak at length without interruption and looking attentive while they are speaking. The longer they speak, the more respect is given to them. It is very important that a person who feels entitled to respect is not contradicted in front of others. If a criticism is made, it may well be interpreted as a declaration of hostility.

As a guest you are in a special category, and entitled to respect. You will find that the people are invariably polite and anxious to agree with what you say. It is possible therefore, that you may regard an appointment as being settled, and then find that no one turns up to meet you. If this happens it is important not to get angry, because failure to show up does not imply any dislike. Rather that, though unable to come, they wished to avoid the confrontation entailed in refusing, and chose the solution which caused the minimum of embarrassment for both sides.

The way to avoid misunderstandings is to think not of what is apparent on the surface but what is lying beneath. Every person in the room with you, whether in a village or in a business meeting in a town, is acting according to the likely effect the discussion will have on them or their relations with others. Outsiders who are sympathetic to this way of thinking and careful to show respect where it is due will quickly be accepted.

PUBLIC HOLIDAYS

There are public holidays on 1 January, 23 April, 30 August, and 29 September. There are also religious holidays marking the end of *Ramazan* and the annual feast of sacrifice which takes place some weeks later. The exact dates vary according to the lunar calendar, but they can be obtained by telephoning the nearest Turkish Embassy.

Christmas is not celebrated. It is not a good idea to send Christmas cards or presents. Sending New Year cards is becoming more common, and can be a useful way to keep in contact.

BUSINESS IN TURKEY

Turks work from Mondays to Fridays, usually starting at nine in the morning and working until five or six at night. Lunch they take at about midday. Most people take their annual holidays during the hottest part of the year in July and August. The holiday period is not a favourable time to conduct business nor are the first few days of the fast at *Ramazan*. Then, tempers are often very thin because those who are fasting have not yet become accustomed to the change in body rhythm.

Dress should be smart

Business transactions are seen as partly to do with finance, and partly to do with building up a relationship over a number of years. If a Turkish firm buys equipment from you, they may feel that they have a right to expect you to take on some trainees the following year. Or they may ask you to bring some special piece of equipment or tool with you next time you come to Turkey. If negotiations are not going well, think in terms of the possibilities of such contact in the future that you are offering the Turkish side.

There are complex regulations concerning the amount of property a foreigner may own in Turkey, and equally complex regulations governing the tariffs on importing and exporting. The best way to overcome these is to develop close ties with a local individual or firm and ask them to explain the step to take in each case. The nearest Turkish Embassy may be able to help with specific queries. Points concerning the EEC and the current situation regarding tariff barriers should be addressed to:

> The Turkish Desk,
> Direction G,
> The European Commission,
> 200, Rue de la Loi,
> Brussels 1049,
> Belgium.

Business cards are very widely used. Be punctual for business appointments; occasionally it happens that the visitor, anxious to be as relaxed as the locals, arrives half an hour late, whilst the host, anxious not to appear inefficient, turns up exactly on time.

APPEARANCE

Dress should be smart; Turkish businessmen and civil servants always dress in a suit and tie. Clothes can be bought locally but extreme care should be taken as to the quality of the garment. One cannot trust a particular shop because each seems to be supplied by a number of sources which vary from week to week.

When having a haircut, allow ample time, because it is a mark of respect to the client for the hairdresser to be fastidious concerning the final result. Shaving, which is almost entirely done with a cut-throat razor, takes more than half an hour and several glasses of tea. It is appropriate to leave a tip of about ten per cent for the man who did the cutting, and rather less for the boy who takes the coat.

Travelling in Turkey

Istanbul

Most visitors at some point in their stay make a trip to Istanbul. Walking around the city is an extraordinary experience, giving one a sense of how life must have been under the Ottoman Empire, with its sultans, harems, lavish palaces and huge mosques. Alongside this lies evidence of the Byzantine past, in particular the church of Holy Wisdom, *Haghia Sofia*, the frescoes of St Saviour in Chora and the remains of the Hippodrome, where chariot races used to be disrupted by rioting.

The best way to get to know the city is by a combination of walking and using different forms of public transport. The old city lies on a small peninsula between the Bosphorus and the Golden Horn. The Sultan's Palace, *Topkapı Sarayı*, the covered bazaar, *Kapalı Çarşısı*, the Blue Mosque, *Sultan Ahmet*, and most of the Byzantine remains are situated there. On the other bank of the Golden Horn are the old merchants' quarters and the modern part of the city. Across the Bosphorus is a splinter part of the city which is linked by frequent ferry crossings. The visitor will probably begin in the old quarter of the city, and then walk down to Galata Bridge, across the Golden Horn, and along Istiklal Avenue to Taksim Square, the heart of the modern city.

Topkapi interior

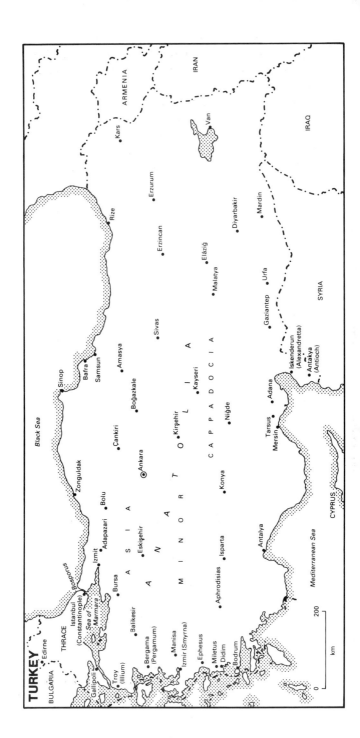

The streets are quite peaceful and assault is uncommon. Unfortunately, though men may look around all day without experiencing the slightest discourtesy, women on their own tend to be harangued in a most unpleasant way. *Defol!* 'Clear off!' said very firmly is the most likely word to achieve results.

As well as normal taxis there are collective taxis, *dolmuş*. *Dolmuş* literally means 'stuffed' and, as this implies, they only set off when full. The routes and fares are fixed by the municipality. Each person passes his fare to the driver by means of the person in front, so it is quite likely that someone will tap you on the shoulder and wave money under your nose. In that case tap the person in front of you on the shoulder and pass the money on. Any change will be passed back by the passengers in the same way. There are buses, but they are usually rather crowded.

All around the city are little restaurants which have the dishes ready cooked and set out in view. This is very convenient, for one simply points to what one wants. The normal way of eating would be to take a main dish with rice, *pilav*, and perhaps yoghurt mixed with water, *ayran*, to drink. There is no need to give a tip. Be very polite with the proprietor, because the bill may vary according to how much he likes you. I returned for the same particularly good soup to a restaurant several days running, and each day as they began to get to know me better the price dropped by about twenty per cent, until in the end I was paying less than half than on the first day.

Baker's boy

One of the most enjoyable aspects of wandering around the city is to see the wealth of street traders. Boot-blacks are everywhere. They put a shine on shoes, but their materials are not to be trusted. In particular avoid them in the rainy season, for the base they use (which they then tint according to the colour of the shoe) often turns white on getting wet.

Another established group sell bread, sweets and cakes. The best of these are *simit*, rolls of bread topped with sesame seeds (see illustration above) which when hot are delicious. To have a drink with them go to a *bufe*; soft-drink bars which specialise in freshly-squeezed fruit juices such as carrot, apple, orange and banana. They also sell *ayran*, yoghurt mixed with salt and water, which is extremely refreshing in warm weather.

Seljuk Fortress, Alanya

TRAVELLING IN THE COUNTRYSIDE

The normal way to travel long distances is by coach. There are many different companies, the best of which are rapid, efficient and have the latest models. Most towns have a terminal. At the terminal, take care not to be pressurised into buying a ticket before checking when the bus goes and what route it runs on. The terminals are crowded, hot and it is easy to lose one's temper. It is better to remain calm until it seems absolutely necessary to state one's case more firmly. Never offer physical violence; if a little fuss is not successful the likelihood is that what you want really is not possible.

Almost half the population of Turkey lives in the countryside and of the town dwellers many have only recently migrated to the towns.

Many people are proud of their village, claiming that its water is clean, the setting beautiful and the hospitality second to none. Indeed it is true that if you go to a village it is likely you will be pressed to eat, drink and even stay the night. Village life is more formal than the town, so that if you accept you will find the rules of showing respect to elders and to guests are especially marked.

On entering a house it is normal to take off one's shoes. In villages, the Islamic greeting *selamünaleykum*, peace be with you!, is customary. If someone has said *selam* to you it is extremely impolite not to return it with the appropriate reply, *aleykumselam*, peace be upon you! You may prefer to initiate a greeting with the more secular *merhaba*! Hello!

Village life

THE SEPARATION OF THE SEXES

Do not be surprised if you only see men. Village life has retained the traditional separation between the sexes. Women may enter only briefly to wish you welcome. The men of the visiting party should take care not to address a woman directly, nor look too long at them. Of course it would be folly to make a pass at a village woman, and likely to result in violence. Women visitors have rather more choice. They may stay with the men as guests, or depart with the village women to their quarters. They may find this a fascinating opportunity to learn something of village life, because village women on their own tend to be less tied down to the formality which characterises male behaviour.

On leaving do not offer money, for this shames the village's hospitality. If you have in your bag a few pieces of good quality, brightly coloured cloth then the women would appreciate this as a gift. An easier way to reciprocate is to take photographs and send them to the village. Men usually do not mind being photographed. Village women will probably be delighted but the only tactful method is for the women of the visiting party to take photographs when there are no males present. Be careful only to take obviously harmless pictures, for example of village life, and of course never near borders or military establishments.

5

Forms of Address

Just as in the West, Turkish names consist of a given name and a family name. In order to address a person respectfully in conversation add after the given name *bey* if a man and *hanım* if a woman. *Hanım* implies that the woman is married, there is no specific term for an unmarried woman. When writing, place *sayın* before the full name whether a man or woman. So, to address a *Mehmet Şimsek* in conversation you would say *Mehmet bey*, when writing a letter to him you would say *Sayın Mehmet Şimsek*. To address a married woman *Deniz Uzunboylu* you would say *Deniz hanım* when speaking, but *Sayın Deniz Uzunboylu* when writing. One of the reforms which has not become widespread but is in use in banks and in civil service offices is to place *bey* or *beyan* in front of the name, e.g. *bey Mehmet Simsek* and *beyan Deniz Uzunboylu*.

WRITING A LETTER

When writing a letter you may write in English on the grounds that the person to whom you address it can find a translator. The address, however, must be written correctly. The name comes first, followed by the street, the number of the building in the street, and then the number of the apartment within the building. After this comes the name of the apartment, the district and the town. *Sayın* is usually abbreviated to *Sn*, *Sokak*, meaning 'street', to *Sok*, *Apartment* to *Apt*. Zipcodes have recently been introduced but they are not necessary. If used, they are usually added after the district.

Sn. Mehmet Akıllı	name
Dar sok. 24/10	name of street and number
Ufak apt.	name of apartment
Kavaklıdere 91030	district and zipcode
Ankara	town

To address a letter to a village it is enough to have the person's name, village (*köy*), sub-province (*ilçe*), and province (*il*). Thus:

Sn Mehmet Akıllı	name
Yesil Köyü	village
Akpınar	sub-province
Malatya	province

Other relevant Turkish words are *adı* - name; *soyadı* - surname; *adres* - address; *mahalle* or *semt* - district; *kent* - town; *şehir* - city; *ülke* - country. Useful words when filling out forms are *memleket* - country of origin; *doğum tarihi* - date of birth; *meslek* - profession.

6
Shopping/ Where to Stay

Istanbul hotel

Finding a place to stay is rarely a problem. Istanbul has several hotels of international standard, the most established being the Hilton (Cumhuriyet Caddesi, Harbiye). More modern are the Sheraton (Taksim Parkı, Taksim) and the Etap Istanbul (Meşrutiyet Caddesi, Tepebaşı). The Pera Palas hotel (Meşrutiyet Caddesi 98-100), built to celebrate the coming of the Orient Express has the most atmosphere. All these hotels are found above Pera, in the modern part of the city.

Cheaper establishments of vastly differing standards are situated across the Golden Horn, close by the Blue Mosque. Some are acceptable and pleasantly furnished (though it is always wise to check the plumbing facilities), others are very basic. There are several youth hostels in this area, which should be treated with some caution, as in spite of the official-sounding name, they are privately run and often not up to scratch.

The pattern is similar for other large cities. Ankara, which previously lacked good hotels, now has two which are very attractive; the Hilton and the Sheraton, both in Gazios-manpaşa. Lower-priced ones are situated in Ulus, the heart of the old quarter. The hotels in Ulus are a good introduction to the facilities to be expected outside the tourist areas. Almost all towns have hotels, usually situated near the market square, but they cater mainly for Turkish people. Rooms are sparsely furnished, often with no more than a bed in them. Toilets are likely to be the squat-style. However, the service is invariably cheerful and friendly and the bed usually comfortable.

WHAT TO BUY

Almost anything available in the West can also be found in Turkey. The problem is that it is usually found in two versions; one made locally (*yerli*) and the other imported (often known as foreign, *yabanci*). Imported goods are substantially more expensive than local ones, so when buying anything be careful that you are paying the appropriate price. The quality of locally-made products varies. Broadly, electrical goods, textiles and common pharmaceuticals are of a reasonable quality. Turkish stationery is very poor, and it is best to take a supply of writing paper with you. Turkish cheeses and wines are often very good. Local vodka (*vodka*), gin (*cin*) or cognac (*konyak*) made under the government monopoly (*tekel*) are not recommended, and possibly even harmful.

Turkey has a wide selection of reasonably-priced traditional goods and crafts. Leather goods, carpets, rugs, copperware and onyx are all made to a very high standard. There are several places to buy them. Sometimes a particular town specialises in making one particular product. Alternatively, a variety of traditional crafts are sold through outlets run by the Ministry of Tourism in most large cities and tourist towns. This is probably the surest way to gain value for money, as both quality and price are controlled but the most enjoyable place to buy goods is in a bazaar, although this means being prepared to bargain to obtain a good price.

BARGAINING

The price of products made under government monopoly are fixed. These include cigarettes and alcohol. In most modern shops the price of goods is clearly marked and bargaining is not acceptable. In the markets and covered bazaar bargaining is the norm. There is no necessary connection between the worth of the goods offered and the price demanded. Thus even if you offer half the quoted amount you still may be offering more than the fair price. In order to escape this problem it is a good idea to wait until you have a feel of the going rates. At all times, do not be hurried by the vendor, do not be afraid of refusing to buy if you feel the price is still too high, and have a look at the produce of several sellers before buying anything.

7

The Language

Street signs

Turkish has been written in the Roman alphabet since the early years of the Republic. It is regular, and not at all linked to Arabic, though there are loan words. The biggest obstacle at the beginning is the strange vocabulary, followed closely by its rather unusual grammar. The key idea is that the root of a verb or noun does not change and inflexions are added to it to express case, tense or person. This may seem a little difficult to get used to, but once grasped almost any situation can be expressed simply and precisely. Thus *gelmek* = to come; *-mek* is the usual infinitive ending. To say 'I am coming' one takes the stem *gel*, and adds to this the sign for the present tense *iyor* and that of the first person singular - *m* to make *geliyorum*. Complicated constructions are outside the scope of this book, but it is worth stressing that the friendly response from the people on whom one tries out one's efforts amply repays the trouble taken in learning.

POLITE WORDS AND PHRASES

merhaba	— hello
lütfen	— please
teşekkür ederim	— thank-you
sağ ol!	— health be! (informal way of expressing thanks)
iyi günler	— good day
iyi geceler	— good night
iyi akşamlar	— good evening
günaydin	— good morning
afiyet olsun!	— good appetite (said both before and after a meal)
af ederseniz	— excuse me
özer dilerim	— sorry
nasılsınız?	— How are you?
iyiyim; siz nasılsınız?	— I'm well; how are you?

VOCABULARY

evet	— yes
hayır	— no
yok	— none, no
çok	— very
çok pahalı	— very expensive
çok uçuz	— very cheap
güzel	— beautiful
fena	— bad

iyi	—	good
kahve	—	coffee, coffee-house
çay	—	tea
bira	—	beer
sarap	—	wine
seker	—	sugar
su	—	water
ekmek	—	bread
yumurta	—	egg
peynir	—	cheese
tuz	—	salt
hesap	—	bill
büyük	—	big
küçük	—	small
yavaş yavaş	—	slowly
çabuk	—	quick
yeter	—	enough
defol!	—	clear off!
buraya gel!	—	come here
burda	—	just here
orda	—	over there
kapalı	—	closed
açik	—	open

PHRASES

istiyorum	—	I want
istemiyorum	—	I don't want
çay istiyorum	—	I want tea
çay istemiyorum	—	I don't want tea
etsiz yemek istiyorum	—	I want food without meat

More politely:

çay lütfen	—	tea, please
etsiz yemek lütfen	—	food without meat please
içdim	—	I have drunk
yedim	—	I have eaten
iyi yedim	—	I have eaten well

gördüm	— I have seen
ödedim	— I have paid
var mı?	— Is there?
ekmek var mı?	— Is there bread?
ne kadar?	— how much?
nerelısınız?	— Where are you from?
Inglizim	— I am English
Amerikalıyım	— I am American
İstanbul'a gitmek istiyorum	— I want to go to Istanbul
Ankara'ya gitmek istiyorum	— I want to go to Ankara

NUMBERS

1	—	*bir*
2	—	*iki*
3	—	*üc*
4	—	*dört*
5	—	*beş*
6	—	*altı*
7	—	*yedi*
8	—	*sekiz*
9	—	*dokuz*
10	—	*on*
11	—	*on bir*
12	—	*on ikı*
20	—	*yirmi*
30	—	*otuz*
40	—	*kırk*
50	—	*elli*
60	—	*altmış*
70	—	*yetmiş*
80	—	*seksen*
90	—	*doksan*
100	—	*yüz*
1,000	—	*bin*
1,000,000	—	*milyon*

Did You Know..?

Modern Turkey took shape in the years after the First World War, gaining recognition from the Western powers at the Treaty of Lausanne signed on 24 July 1923. It was not an easy struggle. A nationalist movement in Ankara, led by Mustapha Kemal (later known as Atatürk), repulsed invasion by Greeks in the west, Italians and French in the south, surpressed uprisings by the Kurds and the Armenians in the east and threatened the allies occupying Istanbul with conflict in the city itself before they gained acceptance of their right to self-government.

The Republic is quite different from the Ottoman Empire. Its capital is Ankara, not Istanbul. Rather than being ruled by a Sultan, sovereignty is vested in a Grand National Assembly, the sole legislative authority. Islam, the basis of the Ottoman state, is disestablished and now has little power to affect the governing of the country.

The Arabic script, in which Ottoman was written has been replaced by the Latin alphabet. The Turkish language has been purged of words of Arabic or Persian derivation, and new words invented to take their place.